THE POWER OF COMMUNICATION IN RELATIONSHIPS

By

Mila Rogers

TABLE OF CONTENTS

INTRODUCTION

Communication is often considered the foundation of any successful relationship. Whether in marriage, romantic partnerships, or long-term commitments, the way we communicate with our loved ones can either strengthen or break the bond between us. But communication is more than just the exchange of words, it's about the ability to listen, understand, and truly connect on a deeper level. In this chapter, we'll explore why communication is the cornerstone of lasting love, and how mastering it can transform not only how you talk but how you connect and grow together.

Communication Isn't Just Talking, It's Reaching

Think about a moment when someone really heard you. Not just nodded politely or waited for their turn to speak, but paused, leaned in, and gave you their full attention. Maybe it was during a time when you were feeling overwhelmed, or maybe you were trying to explain something that mattered to you and weren't sure how it would come across. That moment, when someone didn't just listen but actually understood you, that's the heart of meaningful communication.

In romantic relationships, this kind of communication is more than just helpful; it's essential. Because love isn't sustained by grand gestures or the occasional kind word, it's built, quietly and steadily, in the everyday moments where two people choose to really see and hear each other.

And yet, we're often taught to focus on expressing ourselves, getting our point across, or solving problems quickly. What we don't always learn is how to stay present when our partner speaks, how to listen without forming a rebuttal in our head, or how to ask questions that invite vulnerability instead of shutting it down.

Real communication isn't about winning, it's about connecting.

Why We Miscommunicate (Even with People We Love)

It's strange, isn't it? We can love someone deeply, share our lives with them, and still miss them completely in a conversation.

This happens for a number of reasons. Sometimes we assume we know what they mean. Sometimes we're distracted, or tired, or carrying our own emotional weight that clouds how we interpret what they say. And sometimes we speak through layers, of pride, fear, or old wounds, so even our words come out guarded or distorted.

For example, one partner might say, "You never help around the house," when what they really mean is, "I'm feeling overwhelmed and I need to know we're in this together." But that's not what gets said. And the other partner hears criticism and feels defensive instead of seeing the underlying need for connection and support.

When we don't take the time to slow down and explore what's underneath the words, we miss what's really being said.

Good communication is as much about what's not being said as what is.

The Power of Emotional Safety

One of the most underrated parts of communication is creating emotional safety. This is the invisible container that holds the relationship together, the sense that no matter what's shared, it will be met with respect, care, and curiosity instead of judgment or dismissal.

Without emotional safety, even honest conversations can feel dangerous. You might find yourself filtering your truth, shrinking back, or avoiding topics that need attention. Over time, this creates emotional distance. You might still talk about plans or logistics, but the deeper conversations, the ones about feelings, fears, dreams, or disappointments, start to fade.

Creating emotional safety doesn't mean you have to agree with everything your partner says. But it does mean showing up in a way that communicates: "I care about your heart. I'm not here to tear you down. I want to understand."

It's not always easy. Especially when emotions run high or past hurts get triggered. But in those moments, the way you respond can either deepen your connection or slowly chip away at trust.

Sometimes, just saying, "I can see this really matters to you. Help me understand," can soften the room in ways that no logic or argument ever could.

Listening to Understand, Not to Fix

A common trap many of us fall into, especially in loving relationships, is the urge to fix. You hear your partner struggling and you want to offer solutions, advice, or a way to make it all go away. This comes from a good place, but it can unintentionally make the other person feel unheard.

Sometimes, your partner isn't asking for answers. They're asking for presence. They want to know they're not alone in what they're feeling.

This means resisting the urge to jump in with "Have you tried...?" or "Well, at least..." and instead simply saying things like:

"That sounds really hard."

"I can imagine that felt really frustrating."

"I'm here with you."

This kind of listening creates intimacy. It's the experience of being emotionally held, of knowing someone sees your pain and doesn't try to clean it up or make it smaller.

There's a healing in that kind of presence. And it's the kind of communication that builds lasting love, not just in the easy times, but especially in the hard ones.

Speaking Honestly Without Blame

Of course, good communication isn't just about listening. It's also about speaking, with clarity, honesty, and kindness. That's not always easy. Especially when emotions are high.

But there's a difference between saying, "You're always so selfish," and saying, "When you cancel our plans at the last minute, I feel unimportant and hurt."

The first triggers defensiveness. The second invites understanding.

Using "I" statements instead of "You" accusations helps shift the tone of the conversation. It grounds your message in your own experience instead of making it an attack on someone else's character.

This doesn't mean you can't express frustration or hurt. But when you do, try to make space for both truth and grace. Try to leave room for repair, for dialogue, for change.

Timing and Tone Matter

Sometimes it's not what we say, but when and how we say it that determines how it lands.

Bringing up a heavy topic when your partner is exhausted or distracted might backfire, not because the topic isn't valid, but because the space isn't right.

It's okay to say, "I want to talk about something important, can we pick a time when we can really focus on each other?

Tone also plays a huge role. A gentle tone invites openness. A harsh one builds walls. And while we all slip up from time to time, being mindful of the emotional texture of our voice can make a big difference in how safe and loved our partner feels during a conversation.

Repairing After Miscommunication

No matter how skilled we become at communication, we're still human. We'll still get it wrong sometimes. We'll say the wrong thing, speak too sharply, miss the point, or shut down when we should've stayed open.

What matters most in those moments isn't perfection, it's repair.

Repair looks like circling back. Like saying, "I didn't show up well earlier. I want to try again." It's choosing humility over pride, and connection over being right.

Couples who know how to repair are often stronger than couples who never argue. Because they've built resilience. They've shown each other that even when things get hard, they can find their way back to each other.

The Little Things Count

While big conversations are important, love is often nurtured in the small, everyday exchanges.

A warm "Good morning." A thoughtful "How was your day?" A text that says, "Thinking of you." These may seem insignificant, but they add up. They create a rhythm of connection—a kind of emotional oxygen that keeps the relationship breathing.

Don't underestimate the power of small moments. They often speak louder than grand declarations.

Growing Together Through Communication

As we grow and change, our relationships do too. That means communication has to grow with us.

The way you connected when you first met might not be what you need now. Life brings new challenges, careers, children, health struggles, loss, transitions, and with those changes come new needs, fears, and hopes.

Regular check-ins can help you stay in sync. Not just about logistics, but about how you're both doing emotionally. Questions like:

"What's been on your heart lately?"

"Is there anything I can do to support you better?"

"How are we doing, really?"

These questions keep the lines open. They help you keep learning each other, even after years together. And they remind you that communication isn't a one-time skill—it's an ongoing practice of love.

CHAPTER ONE

UNDERSTANDING TRUE COMMUNICATION IN RELATIONSHIPS

When we think about communication in a relationship, we often imagine long heart-to-hearts at the kitchen table, passionate conversations, or honest confessions that lead to breakthroughs. But real, effective communication is more than words. It's about presence. It's about connection. It's about the emotional current flowing underneath the dialogue, the unspoken "do you see me?" and the quiet hope that the answer is "yes."

Many couples fall into the trap of thinking that as long as they're talking, they're communicating. But talking isn't always the same as connecting. You can talk for hours and still walk away feeling misunderstood, unseen, or emotionally alone. That's the painful part, when words are exchanged, but hearts aren't reached.

It's not what you say, it's how you say it, and more importantly, how it's received.

We all come into relationships with our own emotional wiring, shaped by past experiences, upbringing, and even past hurts. So while one partner might crave detailed conversations and verbal reassurance, the other might prefer quiet presence or physical closeness as their form of expression. Neither is wrong—but without clear, attuned communication, both can feel like they're speaking different languages.

What complicates things further is the assumption that love should equal mind-reading. "They should know I'm upset." "If they loved me, they'd understand." But no matter how emotionally attuned someone is, they're not a mirror image of you. They don't know what's swirling in your mind unless you offer them the roadmap. And that roadmap, your inner emotional world, needs to be shared with clarity, with care, and with the willingness to be vulnerable.

True communication often requires slowing down. Not rushing to defend. Not rehearsing your reply while your partner is still speaking. But really tuning in, listening with your heart rather than your head. When both people feel seen and safe enough to be honest, even messy conversations can become moments of deep intimacy.

Why Communication Is the Key to Emotional Needs

Every human being carries invisible needs. Some are simple, like "I need to feel appreciated." Others are deeper, "I need to feel safe with you. I need to trust that you care, even when I mess up. I need to know you really hear me."

In relationships, emotional needs are met, or missed, through the way we communicate.

Take a common scenario: You're feeling overwhelmed and distant from your partner. Instead of saying, "I'm feeling disconnected and could use some closeness," you snap, "You never make time for me." On the surface, it sounds like frustration. But underneath, there's a tender, unmet need: Please notice me. Please choose me again.

Now imagine being on the receiving end of that. It's hard to hear the real need behind the sharp tone. Instead, the defence walls go up: "I do spend time with you. What are you even talking about?" And just like that, two people who love each other are now locked in a cycle of misunderstanding.

The sad part? Both want the same thing, to feel valued, loved, and connected. But the way it's communicated gets tangled in tone, timing, or emotional residue from past arguments.

The challenge, and opportunity, is in learning to express emotional needs before they boil over into criticism or shutdown. Saying something like, "I'm feeling a little distant from you and I'd love to reconnect, maybe we could spend some time together tonight?" sounds simple, but it takes awareness, humility, and sometimes, unlearning old patterns of self-protection.

When couples develop the ability to communicate their emotional needs without blame, it transforms the relationship. It creates a climate of emotional safety where both people feel invited into each other's world. And in that kind of space, healing happens. Closeness grows. Love deepens.

The Communication Cycle: How Disconnection Grows, and How to Change It

Let's be honest, most of us don't learn how to communicate in emotionally intelligent ways growing up. We absorb what we see. Maybe it was yelling. Maybe it was silence. Maybe it was sarcasm, avoidance, or pretending everything was fine.

So, in adulthood, we find ourselves repeating patterns. One person shuts down, the other pursues. One avoids conflict, the other needs to talk it out right now. And if those patterns aren't recognized, they become a cycle, a dance of disconnection that can feel impossible to stop.

Here's how it often plays out: One partner feels neglected and brings it up, perhaps clumsily. The other, feeling attacked, deflects or defends. The first partner gets louder or colder. The second partner withdraws. Rinse, repeat.

Sound familiar?

Now flip the script. What if, instead of reacting, one partner paused and responded differently? Imagine this:

Your partner says, "I feel like you don't care anymore. You're always busy."

Instead of snapping back, you breathe and say, "That's hard to hear. Can you tell me more about how I've been coming across lately?"

That single shift, from defensiveness to curiosity, can break the cycle.

It doesn't mean the conversation will be easy. But it changes the tone. It opens the door to honesty without combat. It says, "I'm here. I want to understand." And when both people begin to practice this, even imperfectly, a new cycle begins—one of safety, emotional availability, and mutual care.

Active Listening: The Foundation of Effective Communication

If there's one skill that could radically transform your relationship, it's active listening. And not the kind where you nod and wait your turn to talk. I'm talking about the kind of listening that makes the other person feel like they truly matter.

Here's what active listening looks like in real life:

- You put the phone down. Not just physically, but mentally. Your attention shifts fully to your partner, even if only for a few minutes.
- You let them finish their thought. Even if you disagree. Even if you're itching to clarify or correct. You wait.
- You reflect what you hear. "So, what I'm hearing is that you felt dismissed when I brushed off your concern earlier. Is that right?" This one step alone can defuse tension, because being understood is half the battle.
- You tune in to the emotion beneath the words. Sometimes, what your partner is saying isn't the whole story. A sarcastic remark might hide pain. A sigh might signal exhaustion. Listening with empathy means you're paying attention to more than just the surface.

- You ask, not assume. "Help me understand, what was it about that moment that hurt you the most?" Questions like this show humility and willingness to learn.

Active listening isn't about fixing. It's about presence. Often, the person you love doesn't want a solution. They want to feel like they're not alone in their struggle. They want to feel held, emotionally. And when they do, connection blooms again.

Creating a New Communication Culture

At the heart of all of this is a simple but powerful truth: We all want to feel close, safe, and loved in our relationships. Communication is the vehicle that gets us there—or keeps us stuck.

So, if you're reading this and thinking, "We've messed this up too many times," take a breath. You're not alone. And more importantly, you're not doomed.

Changing how you communicate isn't about getting it perfect. It's about practicing small shifts, over and over:

- Pausing before reacting.
- Checking in gently instead of accusing.
- Saying, "I need," instead of "You never."

Listening like it's the most important thing in the world, because in that moment, it is.

The more you practice these things, the more natural they become. And over time, they become the culture of your relationship. A place where both people feel known, supported, and free to be fully themselves.

And isn't that what we all want?

Nonverbal Communication: The Silent Language

It's strange how often we think of communication as something that happens only through words, as if language alone is responsible for the depth and clarity of our connections. But the truth is, some of the most powerful messages we send to one another happen without a single syllable. In fact, studies suggest that up to 93% of communication is nonverbal. That's huge. It means that even when we think we're being clear with our words, our bodies, our faces, and our tone might be telling an entirely different story.

Think about the last time someone told you they were "fine," but their tone was flat, their arms were crossed, and they couldn't quite meet your eyes. Did you believe them? Probably not. Because everything about their posture and expression contradicted their words. And in moments like that, our intuition kicks in. We feel the truth before we even understand it logically.

That's the beauty, and complexity, of nonverbal communication. It's raw, instinctive, and incredibly revealing.

Let's bring this into real life for a moment. Imagine you're in the middle of a heated conversation with your partner. Maybe something small spiralled into something bigger, and now you're both frustrated. You say you're "listening," but your arms are folded, your body is angled away, and you haven't looked them in the eye for five minutes. Whether you realize it or not, your body is sending a signal: I'm not open right now. I'm defending myself. I'm protecting something.

And your partner feels that. Even if they can't articulate it, they feel the wall.

Now flip it. What happens when you uncross your arms, take a deep breath, and soften your shoulders? What happens when you turn toward them, make gentle eye contact, and nod as they speak, even if you don't fully agree with them yet? Something shifts. The tension drops. They feel seen, heard, acknowledged. It's subtle, but the impact is huge.

Our nonverbal signals act as the tone behind the words, giving them weight and intention. A soft tone can de-escalate conflict. A smile can invite warmth. A hand on the shoulder can say, "I'm here," even when the words feel stuck. And sometimes, when emotions are running high and words just won't come out right, those unspoken gestures matter most.

But here's the catch, nonverbal communication isn't always intentional. We often send messages without meaning to, especially when we're emotionally overwhelmed. That's why self-awareness is key. Tuning into your own body, how it reacts, where it tenses, what it's silently broadcasting, can help you communicate more clearly and more compassionately.

Ask yourself: What is my body saying right now that my mouth isn't?

It's not about performing or pretending to be open when you're not. It's about bringing integrity between what you feel, what you need, and what you show. The more aligned those are, the easier it becomes for others to trust you, connect with you, and feel safe with you, even in hard moments.

The Role of Emotional Safety in Communication

Let's talk about emotional safety, not the kind of safety that protects you from physical harm, but the kind that lets your guard down, that lets you exhale. It's that deep, invisible comfort we feel when we know we can be fully ourselves with someone. No judgment. No shaming. Just presence, patience, and space to be real.

In a relationship, emotional safety is everything. Without it, conversations get twisted. Vulnerability becomes risky. And honesty starts to feel like a gamble

Emotional safety doesn't mean we'll always agree with each other or that difficult feelings won't arise. It simply means that when they do, we can bring them forward without fear of being ridiculed or rejected. It means we trust that the other person won't weaponize our feelings or throw them back in our face. And that kind of trust takes time, and care, to build.

You might remember a moment when you really opened up to someone. Maybe you shared something you were scared to say aloud, a dream, an insecurity, or a raw emotion. What made that moment possible? Likely, it was the other person's response. Maybe they learned in and listened. Maybe they didn't interrupt or rush to fix it. Maybe they said something as simple as, "Thank you for sharing that." That's emotional safety in action.

And when it's missing? You feel it in your gut. You start rehearsing your words before you speak. You hesitate. You filter. You weigh the risks. And eventually, you might stop sharing altogether, not because you don't care, but because it doesn't feel safe to.

One of the most tender gifts we can give someone we love is a safe space to be fully human. That means welcoming emotions that are messy or uncomfortable. It means listening with curiosity rather than defensiveness. And yes, it means holding space for silence sometimes, because not everything needs to be fixed or solved right away. Sometimes, just being there is enough.

It's easy to think of communication as a skill, something we can master with the right techniques. But emotional safety isn't a technique. It's a way of being. A softness in how we show up. A commitment to staying open, even when it's hard.

And it goes both ways. You deserve emotional safety, too. If you're always the one doing the emotional heavy lifting, holding the space, calming the storm, tiptoeing around someone's reactions, it may be worth asking: Am I emotionally safe in this relationship?

Safety isn't about perfection. We all have moments where we miss the mark, say the wrong thing, or shut down. But when there's mutual care and a shared intention to repair and reconnect, even those missteps can become part of the healing process.

Speaking Heart to Heart

At the core of every strong, resilient relationship is communication, not just the ability to exchange information, but the deeper, more vulnerable act of connecting. Of truly seeing and being seen.

When we learn to pay attention to the silent language of our bodies, to soften our tone, to notice the way we posture ourselves in tense moments, we start to communicate in a more honest and compassionate way. We begin to realize that sometimes, it's not what we say, it's how we say it that matters most.

And when we create emotional safety, for ourselves and for each other, we give our relationships room to breathe. Room to grow. Room to be imperfect, yet beautifully honest.

This doesn't happen overnight. It's a practice. A dance of showing up, tuning in, and responding with care. Some days will be messy. Some conversations will hurt. But even in those moments, there's an opportunity to move closer, to understand each other better, to rebuild trust, to choose love over ego.

So maybe the next time you find yourself in a tough conversation, you'll pause. You'll notice your shoulders, your voice, your breath. You'll ask yourself: Am I creating safety here, or tension? You'll lean in, not just physically, but emotionally. And in doing so, you'll help pave the way for a conversation that doesn't just pass information, but that builds connection.

Because real communication is never just about talking. It's about listening, too. It's about empathy. It's about letting someone know, I see you. I hear you. I'm here, and I care.

And if you can do that, even imperfectly, you're already doing something extraordinary.

CHAPTER TWO

UNDERSTANDING YOUR COMMUNICATION STYLE

We all come into relationships with a unique blend of habits, histories, and ways of expressing ourselves. And at the heart of it all—how we connect, resolve tension, share love, or even just manage daily logistics, is communication. It's one of those words that gets thrown around a lot, but rarely do we slow down enough to ask ourselves: How do I actually communicate? And just as important, how does my partner communicate?

The truth is, the way we speak, listen, respond, and even retreat during conflict is deeply shaped by our personalities, upbringing, and life experiences. Sometimes we're aware of it, and sometimes we're not. But when you take time to understand your own communication style, as well as your partner's—you start to notice patterns that were once just frustrating or confusing. Misunderstandings begin to make sense. Emotional needs come into clearer focus. And slowly, the way you relate starts to shift, not just in words, but in understanding, patience, and love.

This chapter is about that shift.

We'll explore four main communication styles as outlined by Brian Tracy: the Relator, Analyzer, Director, and Socializer. Each style has its strengths and its blind spots. And while most people aren't one-dimensional, we tend to lean more strongly toward one style than the others. By recognizing your dominant style, and learning how to spot your partner's, you'll be better equipped to build bridges instead of walls, especially in those emotionally charged or misunderstood moments.

Let's walk through each one together.

The Relator: The Empathetic Listener

You know that friend who always seems to know the right thing to say when you're upset? Or who notices when something's off, even before you say a word? That's the heart of a Relator. These are the emotionally attuned communicators, the ones who genuinely care, who listen not just to respond, but to understand.

Relators value peace and connection. In relationships, they often play the role of the comforter, the safe place. They're less interested in being right than in being close. And their ability to empathize makes them incredibly supportive partners.

Strengths of a Relator

- They make you feel seen. Really seen.
- Their calm presence often diffuses tension.
- They're excellent at picking up emotional nuances others might miss.

But here's where it gets tricky.

Relators often avoid confrontation. Not because they don't care, but because the idea of conflict feels deeply unsettling. So they might hold back their own needs just to keep the peace. They may say "it's fine" when it's not. Or smile when they're hurting.

If you're in a relationship with a Relator, it's important to create a space where they feel safe sharing even uncomfortable truths. Ask gentle questions. Remind them their voice matters. Be soft, especially in hard conversations. And most importantly—don't confuse their calm demeanour for agreement. Sometimes, silence means they're still processing.

If you are a Relator, pay attention to the moments you shrink yourself to avoid discomfort. Your needs are just as valid as anyone else's. Learning to express them, lovingly, clearly, honestly, is one of the greatest gifts you can give to both yourself and your relationship.

The Analyzer: The Logical Problem-Solver

Where the Relator leads with the heart, the Analyzer leads with the mind. Think of the person who wants to "figure it out" before feeling it out. That's an Analyzer. They approach communication like a puzzle, methodical, careful, fact-driven.

Analysers are excellent at breaking things down. They tend to speak with precision, avoiding exaggeration or emotional drama. In a crisis, they're the ones who stay calm and focus on next steps.

Strengths of an Analyzer

- Clear, logical, and thoughtful communicators.
- Able to step back and assess situations without becoming overwhelmed.
- Reliable in problem-solving and decision-making.

But and this is a big one, Analysers can struggle when emotions are front and centre. Not because they don't care, but because emotions don't always fit neatly into boxes. If their partner is crying, for example, they may rush to "fix" the problem instead of just sitting with the feeling.

If you're in a relationship with an Analyzer, understand that their need for clarity isn't coldness, it's how they make sense of the world. Try not to take their logical tone personally. Instead, meet them halfway: bring your feelings, but also frame them in a way that shows how they affect the bigger picture.

If you are the Analyzer, remember that not everything needs to be solved. Sometimes your partner just needs you to be there, to hear them, even if their words are messy or emotional. Let go of the urge to "fix," and focus on connection. You may find that the heart can hold more answers than the mind.

The Director: The Results-Oriented Communicator

Directors come into conversations with one thing in mind: results. They're the take-charge types, the ones who cut through fluff and get straight to the point. Directors tend to be assertive, confident, and focused on solutions.

In relationships, they often take the lead. They're quick to make decisions, quick to speak up, and not afraid to confront issues head-on.

Strengths of a Director

- They communicate with clarity and purpose.
- They're efficient, direct, and decisive.
- They tend to be natural leaders, especially in crisis moments.

But this strength can also be a stumbling block. Directors can come off as impatient or dismissive, especially when their partner wants to talk through feelings. They may interrupt, rush to conclusions, or unintentionally steamroll the conversation. Emotions that don't seem "productive" may be overlooked.

If you're in a relationship with a director, it helps to be clear and confident in your communication. They respect directness. If something is bothering you, don't beat around the bush, say it plainly. But also, gently encourage them to slow down, to pause and ask, "How are you feeling about this?"

If you are the Director, notice how often you dominate conversations. Are you listening to understand, or just to respond? Is your partner feeling heard, or just managed? Your strength is powerful, but it softens beautifully when paired with patience and empathy.

The Socializer: The Charismatic Communicator

Socializers bring the spark to communication. They're the storytellers, the charmers, the ones who can turn an ordinary dinner into an unforgettable memory. They thrive on connection and energy, and they often have a natural gift for making people feel at ease.

In relationships, Socializers are fun, affectionate, and full of life. They're the ones texting funny memes, planning spontaneous adventures, or starting a dance party in the living room.

Strengths of a Socializer

- Effortlessly build rapport and emotional warmth.
- Can lighten tension with humour or playful perspective.
- Make their partner feel seen, valued, and included.

But sometimes, all that charisma can serve as a distraction. Socializers may avoid serious conversations, especially if they feel heavy. They might change the subject, crack a joke, or simply disengage when things get too intense. And while they're great talkers, they're not always the best listeners.

If you're in a relationship with a Socializer, let the lightness live, but don't be afraid to go deeper. Create space for serious conversations—even if they don't always come naturally. And help them see that vulnerability doesn't have to mean losing joy.

If you are the Socializer, take time to practice being fully present. Not every conversation needs to entertain. Your energy is a gift, but when paired with depth and focus, it becomes magnetic. Learn to sit in silence, to listen fully, to stay with discomfort. That's where trust is built.

Bringing It All Together

The most meaningful communication happens not when we try to "fix" each other, but when we seek to understand. None of these styles is better than the other. They each bring something essential. And chances are, your relationship is a mix, a blend of two different styles that sometimes complement and sometimes clash.

But when you begin to name those patterns, to say, "Oh, you're not ignoring me; you're just processing," or *"You're not being cold; you're trying to be logical", *suddenly, the dynamic changes. You move from frustration to curiosity. From reactivity to compassion.

And maybe, more than anything, that's what understanding communication styles is really about: building the bridge between your heart and theirs.

Because love isn't about saying everything perfectly. It's about learning each other's language, one conversation at a time.

Why Understanding Communication Styles Matters in Relationships

If you've ever walked away from a conversation with your partner feeling like you were speaking two different languages, you're not alone. One of the most common challenges in relationships isn't a lack of love, it's a lack of understanding how each person communicates. The way we express ourselves, especially during emotionally charged moments, can either draw us closer or push us apart. It's not just about what we say, but how we say it, and how the other person receives it.

When we talk about communication styles, we're referring to the natural tendencies people have when they express themselves, process information, and respond to conflict or emotional cues. Some of us are direct and to the point; others prefer a more emotional or empathetic approach. Some people need time to think before they speak, while others process things out loud, in real time. These aren't right or wrong ways of being, they're just different. But in a relationship, those differences can either create harmony or friction, depending on how well we understand and adapt to them.

The Power of Knowing Your Own Style

Understanding your own communication style is like learning to read your own emotional map. It gives you a kind of internal compass. When you know how you typically respond in conversations, especially the hard ones, you're more equipped to express yourself in a way that's both honest and constructive.

Let's say, for example, you're someone who shuts down during conflict. Maybe you retreat, hoping the issue will blow over. That might feel safe to you, but if your partner tends to process things externally and wants to talk through everything right away, your silence could be interpreted as disinterest or avoidance. Without understanding your style, and without communicating that to your partner, it's easy to slip into patterns where both people feel unseen and unheard.

On the flip side, if you're someone who jumps in immediately to solve problems, you might unintentionally bulldoze your partner's need to sit with their emotions first. In both cases, knowing your default tendencies allows you to pause, reflect, and maybe choose a different response, one that better serves the moment and the relationship.

Why Your Partner's Style Matters Just as Much

Knowing your own style is only half the picture. The real magic happens when you begin to understand your partner's communication style too. That's where empathy grows. That's where misunderstandings get cleared up before they spiral into conflict. When you can start to see your partner's words and behaviours through the lens of their style, not yours, you stop taking things so personally. You stop reacting and start responding.

Let's take a practical example. Imagine your partner tends to be very logical and solution-focused. You, on the other hand, are more emotionally expressive. When you bring up a stressful situation at work, you're looking for comfort, reassurance, maybe a hug. But instead, they start offering practical suggestions. "Why don't you talk to your boss?" "Maybe you should start looking for a new role." While they're trying to help in their way, it can feel to you like they're minimizing your feelings. But if you understand that their style is about problem-solving, not emotional avoidance, you can better interpret their intentions. And you can help them understand that sometimes, what you really need first is a listening ear, not a fix.

This mutual understanding allows you both to shift, not to become someone you're not, but to meet each other halfway. That middle ground is where connection lives.

Four Benefits of Understanding Communication Styles

Let's break this down into four real, tangible ways that understanding communication styles strengthens a relationship.

1. Preventing Misunderstandings

Miscommunication is often at the root of conflict—not because someone was trying to be hurtful, but because their message got lost in translation. When you know how your partner processes information or stress, you're less likely to assume the worst.

For instance, if your partner goes quiet during an argument, you might assume they're angry or withdrawing love. But if you know that they simply need time to process before responding, you can give them space without spiralling into insecurity. And in turn, they can reassure you with a simple, "I need a moment to think, but I'm still here."

Understanding each other's styles helps take the edge off tense moments and brings a layer of compassion to interactions that might otherwise feel loaded.

2. Reducing Conflict

Not all conflict is bad. In fact, healthy conflict can lead to growth, clarity, and deeper intimacy. But how we handle conflict makes all the difference. If both people enter a disagreement from a place of understanding, knowing how the other prefers to communicate, it becomes easier to navigate tough conversations without causing lasting harm.

Let's say you know your partner needs time to cool off before talking, but you tend to want to resolve things right away. Instead of pushing for immediate resolution (which might only escalate things), you can give them the breathing room they need. And because you've communicated about this in advance, you don't feel abandoned, they've already reassured you that they'll come back when they're ready.

That kind of mutual respect de-escalates conflict before it even begins.

3. Strengthening Emotional Connection

When we feel heard, understood, and respected, we soften. Our defences drop. And in that softness, emotional intimacy flourishes.

Understanding your partner's communication style is one of the most powerful ways to make them feel seen. It shows that you've paid attention, not just to their words, but to the way they express themselves. It shows that you care enough to adjust your approach, not because you have to, but because you want to love them better.

Think of emotional connection like a bridge. Every time you make the effort to understand your partner's inner world— their fears, their triggers, their hopes—you lay another brick.

Over time, that bridge becomes sturdy enough to carry you both through life's hardest moments.

4. Maximizing Strengths

Each communication style has its own set of strengths. Some people are naturally empathetic; others are incredible problem-solvers. Some are gifted listeners, others are strong leaders. When you learn to appreciate these differences, rather than judge or resist them, your relationship becomes more dynamic, more balanced.

Maybe your partner helps ground you when you're overwhelmed with emotion. Or maybe you help them open up emotionally when they tend to default to logic. Instead of seeing these differences as sources of conflict, you can begin to see them as complementary. You bring out the best in each other.

In a healthy relationship, different communication styles don't clash, they collaborate.

How to Discover Your Communication Style

Getting to know your communication style doesn't require a fancy personality test, just a little self-reflection. Here are some guiding questions to help you explore:

How do I react during conflict? Do I retreat and go quiet, or do I speak up immediately? Do I feel the need to "win" the argument, or do I avoid confrontation altogether?

Do I prioritize emotions or efficiency? When someone shares something vulnerable with me, is my first instinct to comfort them or to fix the problem?

How comfortable am I with emotional expression? Do I enjoy deep, vulnerable conversations, or do I prefer to keep things light and logical?

How do I respond to my partner's needs? Do I listen with empathy? Offer solutions? Try to move on quickly?

Once you have a clearer picture of your own style, it becomes easier to recognize how it plays out in your daily interactions, and how it may differ from your partner's.

Don't stop at self-awareness, though. Make it a shared experience. Sit down with your partner and talk about it. You might say something like, "I've realized that when we argue, I tend to get really quiet, and I think it's because I feel overwhelmed. But I know that sometimes you interpret that as me not caring. Can we talk about how we both experience those moments?"

Conversations like these aren't just about information, they're about intimacy. The more open you are with each other, the more trust builds between you.

Conclusion: It's Not About Changing Who You Are

Understanding communication styles isn't about becoming someone else to please your partner. It's about growing, together. It's about learning how to navigate your differences with empathy instead of frustration.

The truth is, every couple is a mix of quirks, histories, patterns, and preferences. And when you take the time to understand how your partner sees the world, and how you yourself operate, you create the conditions for real connection. Not a perfect relationship, but an honest one. A resilient one.

In the end, love isn't just about how much we care. It's about how well we communicate that care. And when you and your partner learn to speak each other's language, even just a little, you lay the foundation for a bond that can weather just about anything.

Because the goal isn't always to agree. The goal is to understand. And from that understanding, everything else begins to grow.

CHAPTER THREE

THE ROLE OF TONE AND BODY LANGUAGE IN COMMUNICATION

When most of us think about communication, we think about words. We think about what to say, how to say it, maybe even when to say it. But here's the thing, we often underestimate how much of what we communicate has absolutely nothing to do with the actual words coming out of our mouths.

Imagine this: you're talking to someone you care about, and they say, "I'm fine." Now, if those two words are delivered with a warm smile and a gentle voice, you might take them at face value. But if they're muttered in a cold, clipped tone, eyes looking away, arms folded tight across their chest you instantly know something's off. The words didn't change. The message did.

In fact, studies suggest that as much as 93% of our communication is nonverbal. That's tone of voice, facial expressions, posture, gestures, and even how close we stand to someone. These things aren't just extras, they are the message. And in relationships, where trust and connection hinge on more than just dialogue, tone and body language become everything.

This chapter explores how these often-overlooked elements of communication can either nurture emotional intimacy or quietly erode it. Let's unpack how tone and body language work together to shape what we say, and more importantly, what others hear.

The Power of Tone

Let's be honest, most of us have had moments where we said the "right" thing but still ended up in an argument. You thought you were being clear, maybe even kind, but somehow it landed completely wrong.

Why does that happen?

Because tone speaks before the words do.

Tone is the emotional undercurrent of our voice. It's the invisible thread that weaves through our sentences, colouring them with anger, affection, sarcasm, boredom, compassion, or anything in between. Even the exact same phrase can carry wildly different meanings depending on how it's said.

Think about the phrase "What are you doing?"

- Spoken with curiosity: it feels inviting, interested.
- With irritation: suddenly, it feels accusatory.
- With a playful tone: now, it's teasing and light-hearted.

See what I mean? Same words, totally different messages. It's not just what you say, it's the music behind the words.

How Tone Affects Communication

1. **Emotionally Charged Tone**

   We all have our moments. Stress, frustration, exhaustion, these things can slip into our voice without us even realizing. A sharp, sarcastic, or defensive tone might feel justified in the moment, but it sends a loud signal to your partner that they're not safe emotionally.

   Even if your words are technically neutral, the way they're delivered can sting. And when someone feels stung, they're less likely to listen and more likely to shut down or retaliate. Think of a conversation like a dance. If your tone feels like a shove, your partner will instinctively move away, not closer.

2. **Calm and Reassuring Tone**

   On the flip side, a gentle, steady tone is like a soft hand on the shoulder. It tells your partner, I'm here. I'm listening. You're safe with me.

   It doesn't mean you have to sound like a monk all the time. But when you speak with warmth and calm, even difficult conversations can become moments of closeness rather than conflict.

One of the greatest gifts you can offer in communication is to regulate your tone, especially when emotions are high. Because when one person stays grounded, it creates space for both people to feel more secure.

3. Tone of Disinterest

Few things are more painful in a relationship than feeling like the other person doesn't care. A flat or disengaged tone, where there's little inflection or emotion, can send the message that you're bored, annoyed, or just checked out.

Even if that's not your intention, it's how it will be interpreted.

This can be especially damaging in long-term relationships, where routine can sometimes numb our attention. But the truth is, the people closest to us still need to feel chosen, not tolerated. Your tone can either say, I'm here and I value you, or I'd rather be somewhere else. And that difference matters more than we think.

4. Tone in Conflict

Tone becomes especially important during conflict. When tensions rise, we often raise our voices without meaning to. We speak quickly, defensively, maybe even harshly.

But a loud voice rarely leads to being heard.

In fact, it usually does the opposite. It triggers the other person's fight-or-flight response. Their heart rate increases, their brain goes into defence` mode, and suddenly, you're no longer solving a problem, you're just reacting to each other's fear and anger.

But if you can keep your tone steady, even when you're upset, you create room for resolution. It's like saying, I'm frustrated, but I still respect you. I still want us to work through this. That's powerful. And rare.

How to Use Tone Effectively

Tone isn't about performance or being overly careful with your words. It's about intention. When you're aware of the emotional energy behind your voice, you can choose how you show up in a conversation.

Here are a few simple but impactful shifts:

- Pause Before You Speak

  Especially during sensitive moments. Ask yourself, What's the feeling in my voice right now? You might realize your tone is sharper than your words intend.

- Soften Your Delivery

  When talking about emotions or hard topics, aim for warmth. A softer tone makes it safer for your partner to be open, honest, and even vulnerable.

- Match Tone to Content

  If you're sharing something serious, let your tone reflect that seriousness. If it's playful, allow some lightness to shine through. Tone is the emotional context of your message, make sure it aligns.

- Steer Clear of Sarcasm

  Even if you're joking, sarcasm can carry an edge that's hard to read. It might feel like teasing to you but land as a jab to someone else, especially if they're already feeling sensitive.

- Listen to Yourself

  Try recording your voice sometime (even just on a voice memo). You might be surprised at how your tone sounds. This isn't about being self-critical, it's about becoming more aware.

Ultimately, the goal isn't to sound perfect. It's to sound real. And real includes being emotionally present, even when it's uncomfortable.

Beyond Words: The Language of the Body

While tone carries the emotion in our words, body language is often the first thing people notice, even before we say a single syllable.

The way we hold ourselves, the look in our eyes, the direction we're facing, all of these speak volumes. And often, they're saying things we don't even realize.

- **Open vs. Closed Posture:** Are your arms folded or relaxed? Are you facing your partner or turned away? Open posture invites connection. Closed posture can signal distance or defensiveness.
- **Eye Contact:** Not the stare-down kind, but the kind that says, I see you. I'm with you. When we avoid eye contact, it can signal avoidance or discomfort, even if that's not what we mean.

Facial Expressions: A raised eyebrow, a half-smile, a frown, these subtle expressions often convey more emotion than a dozen sentences.

Touch: A gentle hand on the arm, a hug, even sitting closer, all communicate presence and affection in ways that words can't.

Body language is especially powerful in relationships because it's the part of us that's hardest to fake. It reveals what we feel, even when we're trying not to show it. That's why paying attention to your body, and reading your partner's cues, can tell you so much about where each of you stands emotionally.

If words are the shell of communication, tone and body language are its soul. They reveal what's underneath, our intentions, our emotions, our willingness to connect.

We often think that communication is about talking. But true communication is about connecting. And that connection lives not just in what we say, but in how we say it. In the tone that says I care, and the body that leans in instead of away.

So, the next time you find yourself in a conversation, especially one that matters, don't just focus on the words. Tune into the music behind them. Pay attention to the language your body is speaking. Because when tone and body language align with love and respect, your message will land, not just in your partner's ears, but in their heart.

Body Language: The Silent Language of Love

You don't need to say a word to let someone know how you feel. In fact, some of the most powerful messages we send, especially in love, are unspoken. The way we tilt our head, the softening of our gaze, the tension in our shoulders, or even the way we walk into a room, these quiet signals often say far more than our mouths ever could.

That's the strange and beautiful truth about body language: it's always speaking. Even when we try to hide how we feel, our bodies often tell the real story. And in relationships, especially romantic ones, this silent language can be either a bridge or a barrier.

When Your Body Speaks Before You Do

Have you ever walked into the room and felt, without anyone saying a thing, that something was off? Maybe your partner was standing stiffly by the sink, avoiding your eyes. Or maybe they smiled at you, but it didn't quite reach their eyes. That's body language in motion.

While we may use tone to emphasize our feelings, warmth, irritation, love, or hurt, body language often reveals the undercurrent beneath those tones. And when our words and our bodies say different things, it's the body that people usually believe.

That's why becoming aware of our own body language, and tuning into our partner's, is such a powerful step toward deeper connection and emotional safety.

How Body Language Influences Communication

Let's take a look at some of the main ways body language shows up in love and communication. These aren't just theories, they're the little things that shape how safe, seen, and heard we feel in a relationship.

1. **Facial Expressions: The Window to Emotion**
   Our faces tell stories even when our mouths stay quiet.
   Think about how much you can gather from just a look. A subtle frown. The crinkling around the eyes when someone really smiles. A raised eyebrow that says, Really?, without a single word.
   When you're talking to your partner, their face is often the first clue to how they're really doing. Are they smiling with ease, or does their mouth feel tight? Do their eyes look tired, guarded, or perhaps even distant?

Our expressions offer constant updates about our emotional state. If you're sharing something vulnerable, and your partner's expression is soft and attentive, it's comforting. If their face is blank or tense, it might make you feel like you're speaking into a void.

The key is alignment, when your face matches your heart. If you're offering reassurance, let it show in your eyes. If you're upset but trying to pretend otherwise, your partner will sense the disconnect. Let your expressions tell the truth, gently.

2. Posture: Are You Leaning In or Pulling Away?

Our bodies hold tension, but they also reveal where our attention is.

Sitting slouched on the couch while your partner opens up about something important may not feel like a big deal. But that posture, disengaged, turned away, maybe scrolling through your phone, communicates, I'm not really here.

In contrast, leaning in, turning toward them, keeping your body open, these small shifts signal, I care. I'm with you. I'm listening.

Crossed arms? They often say, I'm guarded. I'm not open right now. It doesn't mean you're angry. You might just be cold or tired. But in the moment, your partner may read it as defensiveness or disinterest.

Posture is subtle, but powerful. It's the physical space we offer one another, whether we're making room for closeness or shutting it down.

3. **Eye Contact: Seeing and Being Seen**

Few things create intimacy faster than eye contact. It's where connection happens, where we feel seen—not just looked at, but seen.

Looking into someone's eyes while they're speaking is a way of saying, I value what you're saying. I'm here with you. But it's not just about staring, eye contact, like a dance, needs to feel mutual and natural.

Too little eye contact can feel like avoidance or disconnection. Too much can feel intense or even invasive. The sweet spot is found in a gentle gaze, especially during emotional or vulnerable conversations. Let your eyes soften. Let them reflect presence.

In love, it's often in those quiet moments of shared eye contact where words fall away, and you simply feel each other. It's intimate, grounding, and quietly powerful.

4. **Gestures: The Story Your Hands Tell**

We don't always think about our hands when we're talking. But they're part of the story, too.

A hand placed on a partner's knee, a warm touch on the shoulder, a nod of understanding—these gestures create emotional punctuation. They underline the sentiment behind our words.

On the flip side, clenched fists, tapping fingers, or constant fidgeting can signal anxiety or irritation. It's not about policing your movements, but being aware. If your partner is sharing something painful and you're fidgeting with your phone or distractedly picking at your sleeve, they might feel like you're not fully there.

Gestures aren't just about what you say with your hands, they're about the kind of emotional climate you're creating in that moment.

How to Use Body Language Effectively in Relationships

Being intentional with your body language isn't about becoming robotic or rehearsed. It's about tuning into the emotional resonance of your presence. Here are a few natural ways to invite openness and connection:

- Face your partner during conversations. Literally. Angle your body toward them. It shows attentiveness and respect.
- Keep your arms relaxed and uncrossed. Especially during hard conversations, this communicates, I'm open to hearing you, even if this is hard.

- Use your face as part of your empathy. A gentle smile, a furrowed brow that mirrors concern, or nodding as they speak, these all signal that you're emotionally present.
- Respect physical space. Especially during conflict, give your partner enough room to breathe. Standing too close can feel confrontational, while too much distance might feel cold.
- Mirror without mimicking. Subtly matching your partner's energy or posture can create a feeling of emotional sync. But be careful not to imitate, it should feel organic, not performative.

Tone and Body Language in Conflict: When the Stakes Are High

If there's ever a time when body language really matters, it's during conflict. When emotions are running high, we're more likely to fall back on reactive habits, and often, our bodies do the talking before we even realize it.

How Body Language Can Escalate Conflict

- Raised voices can trigger alarm, even if the words aren't aggressive. The volume alone can shut down connection.
- Crossed arms, turned backs, or rolled eyes send a clear message: I'm not open to you right now. That hurts more than we realize in moments of emotional vulnerability.

- Aggressive gestures like pointing, slamming a hand down, or exaggerated expressions can intensify feelings of being attacked or misunderstood.

The tricky part? We often don't mean to communicate these things. But they still land, and they shape the emotional tone of the conversation.

How to De-escalate Conflict with Body Language and Tone

When things feel tense, the first step is often to soften, not your point, but your delivery.

- Lower your voice. This isn't about silencing yourself. It's about creating space for safety. A calm voice invites calm in return.
- Open your posture. Even if you're frustrated, resist the urge to cross your arms or physically turn away. Stay present.
- Offer a gentle gesture. A soft hand on the arm, if welcomed, can sometimes say I'm still here, and I care, even in disagreement.
- Pause when needed. If the conversation is spiralling, it's okay to step away. Taking a walk, breathing deeply, or just sitting apart for a few minutes can reset the nervous system and allow you both to return in a better headspace.

The Deeper Truth Behind Body Language

At the heart of all this is a simple truth: We want to feel safe with each other. Body language isn't about perfection, it's about presence. When we show up physically in ways that match our emotional intentions, trust begins to take root.

Love isn't just about grand declarations. It's about small, embodied moments of connection: the softening of a glance, the quiet warmth of sitting close, the way we reach for each other in the kitchen without thinking. It's how we hold each other without words.

Tone and body language are often the undercurrent of our communication. They shape how our words are received, how our partner feels in our presence, and how safe we are to be ourselves with each other.

We don't have to get it perfect. But with gentle awareness, we can become better at listening, not just with our ears, but with our eyes, our posture, our presence. And when we do, our love becomes not just something we say, but something we show every, day, in every gesture, in every quiet moment between the words.

CHAPTER FOUR

THE POWER OF EMPATHY AND VALIDATION IN COMMUNICATION

There's something quietly powerful about feeling understood, truly understood, not just heard, but seen, and held in a space where your feelings aren't questioned or brushed aside. In relationships, this kind of understanding is rare, but it's also foundational. It's what we crave when we're hurt, confused, overwhelmed, or even just trying to make sense of our day. At the heart of this kind of connection is empathy and validation. They might sound like soft skills or emotional buzzwords, but in truth, they're the bedrock of trust and intimacy. Without them, communication becomes surface-level. With them, it becomes transformative.

Empathy isn't about having all the answers or saying the right thing, it's about entering into someone else's emotional world without needing to fix or judge it. Imagine sitting beside your partner after a long, draining day. They slump on the couch and say, "I feel like I'm failing at everything." The urge might be to quickly reassure them: "You're not failing." Or worse, to jump in with, "You just need to be more organized." But what if instead, you paused, leaned in a little, and said, "That sounds really heavy. I'm sorry you're carrying so much." That moment, right there, is empathy. It's not a solution. It's connection.

Empathy shows up in different ways, and it's not always dramatic. Sometimes it's quiet: a nod, a soft "I get it," a hand on the shoulder. There are times when it's more of a posture than a response, where your presence says, "I'm here with you." There are three forms empathy tends to take, though they often overlap. Cognitive empathy helps you intellectually understand what your partner might be thinking. Emotional empathy allows you to feel what they're feeling, to get swept up in their joy or ache alongside their pain. And compassionate empathy moves you to act, to step in with a meal, a gesture, or a kind word because you feel their struggle so deeply you can't help but respond.

Each of these forms is important in different moments. During an argument, cognitive empathy can prevent escalation by helping you see that your partner isn't trying to attack you, they're trying to be heard. When they're grieving, emotional empathy lets you share their sorrow without needing to fill the silence. And when life feels overwhelming for them, compassionate empathy becomes the force that helps you ask, "What can I do right now that would make things even just a little easier?"

Empathy strengthens the emotional thread between you. When someone feels deeply understood, they open up. They soften. Their guard comes down, and trust fills the space that defensiveness once occupied. It's in those moments that relationships grow, not when problems are solved, but when hearts are held.

But empathy alone isn't quite enough. It's only half the story. The other half is validation.

Validation is what turns empathy into something that can be felt. It says, "What you feel matters." It doesn't try to compare or correct. It just allows. And that's a powerful gift. Because let's be honest. how many of us grew up in environments where feelings were dismissed with phrases like "Stop being so sensitive" or "There's no reason to be upset"? Those messages, subtle as they may be, teach us to doubt our emotions, to bottle them up, or worse, to feel shame for having them in the first place.

In a healthy relationship, validation undoes that damage. When your partner says, "I felt really ignored when you were on your phone during dinner," and you respond with, "I wasn't ignoring you, I was just checking something important," the conversation often hits a wall. But if you take a breath and say, "I can understand why you'd feel that way, I'm sorry I wasn't more present," something changes. Suddenly, your partner doesn't have to fight to prove their feelings are real. They feel accepted, and that opens the door to genuine repair

Validation creates emotional safety. It tells your partner that they don't have to justify how they feel. They can just be, without needing to earn your approval or edit their truth to fit your comfort level. That kind of freedom is rare, and it's deeply healing.

You might wonder, "But what if I don't agree with how they feel?" That's the beauty of validation, it doesn't require agreement. It just requires presence and respect. You can validate someone's emotions without endorsing their conclusions. You might not think the situation warrants such a strong reaction, but if it feels big to your partner, then it is big to them. And honouring that feeling, instead of minimizing it, is what makes space for closeness.

The hard part, of course, is that empathy and validation ask us to slow down. They ask us to set aside our impulse to fix, defend, or react. They ask us to pause long enough to really listen, not just to the words being said, but to the emotion underneath them. That takes effort. And sometimes, it takes courage. Because when someone we love is in pain, it's uncomfortable. We want to make it go away. We want to lighten the mood, crack a joke, or rush to a solution. But the most loving thing we can do is stay in the discomfort with them and say, "I'm not going anywhere."

There's a moment I remember vividly from a couple I worked with. The wife had just opened up about how isolated she felt staying home with their newborn, while her husband was busy at work. She wasn't angry, just tired and fragile. He could've easily said, "But I'm working hard for us!" Instead, he paused, looked her in the eye, and said, "I had no idea you felt that lonely. I hate that I didn't see it. I want to be better for you." She broke into tears—not because he offered a fix, but because he truly heard her. That's what empathy and validation do. They create space for healing, for reconnection, for grace.

Learning to offer empathy and validation isn't about perfection. You won't always get it right. You'll interrupt, or say the wrong thing, or miss a cue. But the willingness to keep trying—that's what matters. It's in the trying that love becomes a practice, not just a feeling.

Try listening to your partner with the goal of understanding, not responding. Notice the moments when they're not asking for a solution, they're asking for a witness. Catch yourself when you want to say, "That's not what happened," and instead try, "It makes sense that it felt that way to you." And when they express pain or vulnerability, ask yourself: Can I hold this moment without rushing it away?

Because often, what our loved ones want most is not advice, or logic, or even agreement. They want to know that their experience, whatever it is, is valid. That they don't have to shrink it or reshape it to make it palatable. That they are enough, as they are, even in their messiest moments.

Empathy and validation won't solve every problem, but they will change the way you move through problems together. They'll turn tense conversations into moments of closeness. They'll turn conflict into connection. They'll turn your relationship into something that feels like home, safe, honest, and deeply human.

And maybe that's the whole point. Not to avoid hard feelings or disagreements, but to learn how to hold each other through them with gentleness and care. To say, over and over again, in a thousand different ways: I see you. I hear you. You matter to me.

Because when that becomes the language you speak in your relationship, everything changes. Not overnight. Not perfectly. But slowly, quietly, and with the kind of depth that lasts.

Empathy, Validation, and Conflict Resolution

We don't usually plan for conflict in our relationships. It creeps in quietly, often on the heels of fatigue, misunderstandings, or unmet expectations. Suddenly, something as small as a forgotten text or a misunderstood tone spirals into tension. And in that fragile space, words can land like sharp pebbles against a window, rattling, splintering, and sometimes cracking the emotional safety we've worked so hard to build.

But here's the thing most of us forget when we're in the middle of a disagreement: being "right" often isn't the real win. The real victory is staying connected, especially when things are hard. And that's where empathy and validation come in, not as lofty ideals or psychological jargon, but as grounded, everyday tools that can make a world of difference when emotions run high.

Why We Default to Defensiveness

When conflict arises, most of us instinctively move into one of two roles: defender or attacker. Sometimes we're both, alternating between lashing out and justifying ourselves, trying to make sense of our pain by focusing on who's to blame.

This reaction isn't random, it's survival. Our brains are wired to protect us from perceived threats, and emotional pain, especially in intimate relationships, can feel just as intense as physical danger. That's why it's so hard to stay soft when we're hurt. Why our voices rise. Why we might shut down or lash out.

But what if, instead of armouring up, we leaned in?

Empathy and Validation: The Game-Changers

At its core, empathy is about stepping into someone else's emotional shoes, not just understanding what they're feeling, but letting yourself feel with them. It's a quiet, courageous act that says, "I'm here with you, not against you."

Validation, on the other hand, is the art of showing someone that their emotional experience makes sense. Even if you see things differently. Even if you would have reacted another way. It's not about agreeing with their perspective, it's about respecting that it's real to them.

These two tools, empathy and validation, don't magically erase conflict, but they do something just as powerful: they soften it. They create a bridge over the emotional canyon that disagreement can create. They make space for conversation rather than combat.

How They Work in Conflict

Let's say your partner is visibly upset because you forgot an important date, maybe their birthday or your anniversary. You're caught off guard. You had a hectic week, and it completely slipped your mind. The instinct might be to defend yourself:

"I've had so much on my plate. It's not like I don't care, you know that!"

You might even try to minimize their pain:

"It's just a day. We can celebrate tomorrow."

But those responses, while understandable, often make things worse. They communicate this, even if unintentionally: "Your feelings are inconvenient to me."

Now, contrast that with this approach:

"I can see why you're hurt. That day matters to you, and it should matter to me too. I get how my forgetting it would make you feel unimportant."

And then:

"You're completely valid in feeling upset. I'm sorry I let you down like that. I don't want you to feel like you don't matter to me, because you do, so much."

That kind of response doesn't just acknowledge the facts, it meets the person emotionally. And in doing so, it de-escalates the situation. It says, "You're safe to feel what you feel here."

The Power of De-Escalation

When we feel seen, we don't have to yell to be heard.

Empathetic responses help turn down the emotional volume in a conversation. Instead of speaking from a place of defensiveness, they invite vulnerability. You're no longer on opposite sides of a battlefield, you're on the same side, looking at the challenge together.

It's important to remember: validation is not admission of guilt. It's not saying, "I'm 100% wrong, and you're 100% right." It's simply saying, "Your pain is real, and I care about it."

So often in conflict, what people need most is to know their feelings are valid. That they're not "too sensitive" or "overreacting." That someone they love is willing to sit in the discomfort with them, not fix it right away, but just be there.

That presence, nonjudgmental, curious, open, is what empathy looks like in practice.

Creating a Space for Collaboration

Once emotions have settled and both people feel seen, something powerful happens: the conversation shifts from competition to collaboration.

Instead of fighting to be heard, both partners start listening.

Instead of trying to win, they start trying to understand.

That's when solutions feel less like compromises and more like co-creations. It's not about one person giving in. It's about both people asking, "How can we do this better next time? What do we each need to feel more secure, more valued, more understood?"

This kind of problem-solving doesn't come from a checklist. It comes from a felt sense of connection, of knowing your partner is for you, not against you.

Empathy and Validation Build Emotional Intimacy

Here's what we don't talk about enough: emotional intimacy isn't just built in romantic, candlelit moments. It's forged in the fires of hard conversations, when someone could have walked away but didn't. When they could have dismissed your feelings but chose to lean in instead.

Every time you show empathy in conflict, you're saying:

"Even when it's messy, I'm here."

Every time you validate your partner's feelings, you're saying:

"What matters to you, matters to me."

And that message? It lays the foundation for a relationship where both people feel safe enough to be fully human. Imperfect. Emotional. And still, deeply loved.

But What If I Don't Agree?

A common question that comes up is: "How can I validate someone's feelings if I don't agree with their interpretation of what happened?"

That's the beauty of validation—it's not about agreeing with the facts. It's about acknowledging the emotional impact. You can say:

"I can see how that felt really hurtful to you, even though I didn't intend it that way."

That kind of statement keeps the door open. It allows space for both experiences to coexist. You don't have to sacrifice your perspective to honour theirs.

Real-Life Example: A Missed Call and Misunderstanding

Let's paint a real-life scene. You're out with friends, and your partner texts and calls several times, but your phone is in your bag. When you finally check it hours later, there's a message: "Where are you? I've been worried sick."

You call them back, and they're upset, not just worried, but angry.

Your gut reaction might be irritation: "Why are you making a big deal out of this? I just didn't see my phone."

But pause.

Instead, try this:

"I didn't realize how late it had gotten, and I didn't see the calls. I can hear in your voice that you were really worried. That must have been scary, wondering where I was."

Followed by:

"Your feelings are completely understandable. I should've checked my phone, and I'll make sure to be more mindful of that moving forward."

This doesn't require self-blame. It simply acknowledges the reality of how your actions affected them. And that acknowledgment creates space for connection, rather than defensiveness.

The Long-Term Impact

When empathy and validation become habits—not just occasional tools, they transform the very fabric of a relationship.

Conflicts don't magically disappear. But they don't tear you apart, either. They become doorways to deeper understanding. Opportunities to grow closer, not drift further.

Because when people feel emotionally safe, they don't have to guard themselves. They don't have to perform or defend or retreat. They can show up honestly—messy, complicated, tender, and still be met with love.

That's the real power of empathy and validation: they create a relationship where both people can be fully human and still feel fully held.

In Closing

We live in a world that often teaches us to win arguments, to stand our ground, to speak louder. But the truth is, the strength of a relationship isn't in who "wins." It's in who stays. Who listens. Who chooses softness over certainty.

Empathy and validation aren't always easy. They ask us to stretch beyond our egos, to be curious about pain we might not understand, and to love someone through their most unfiltered moments.

But they are worth it.

Because in the end, we're not just trying to resolve a conflict—we're trying to protect the connection. And every time we choose empathy over defensiveness, validation over dismissal, we're quietly whispering:

"This relationship matters. You matter. And I'm not going anywhere."

Coming Up Next...

In the next chapter, we'll dive deeper into how to navigate difficult conversations, those emotionally charged moments that feel like landmines, and how to handle them with grace, honesty, and courage. We'll explore real-world scripts, subtle communication cues, and what it means to truly listen without losing yourself.

Because empathy and validation aren't just tools, they're a way of relating that can help us hold onto each other, even when everything else feels hard.

Let's keep going.

CHAPTER FIVE

NAVIGATING DIFFICULT CONVERSATIONS WITHOUT LOSING CONNECTION

D ifficult conversations can sneak up on us. One moment, everything feels normal, and the next, a single sentence unearths something raw, an old wound, a brewing frustration, or a need that's gone unmet for too long. These aren't just surface-level moments; they strike at the core of what it means to be seen, loved, and respected in a relationship.

Whether you're talking about finances, unmet emotional needs, intimacy, or past hurts, these moments tend to press on vulnerable places. And when that happens, it's easy to shift into fight, flight, or freeze. You either push harder, shut down, or walk away. None of those responses are wrong, they're deeply human. But if we want to build something lasting, we have to learn how to stay present, especially when the conversation feels anything but safe.

This chapter isn't about having "perfect" communication. It's about staying connected, even when it's uncomfortable. It's about learning to see hard conversations not as threats to your relationship, but as doorways into deeper understanding and intimacy. Because the truth is: how you talk during the hard stuff matters more than what you say when things are easy.

The Importance of Respect in Difficult Conversations

Respect sounds like such a basic concept, like something we all assume is already present. But in the heat of a tough moment, respect is often the first thing to go. Frustration builds, words get sharper, tone gets colder. Suddenly, it's not about resolving an issue, it's about winning, being heard louder, or protecting yourself.

But when respect leaves the room, connection follows.

Let's slow it down here. Respect isn't just about being polite. It's about holding space for the whole person in front of you, even when they're saying something hard to hear. It means being mindful of the impact of your words, not just your intentions. And it requires seeing your partner not as the problem, but as someone you love who's struggling alongside you.

Key Aspects of Respectful Communication:

- **No Interrupting:** It's tempting to jump in when you think you've got the answer, or when you feel misunderstood. But when you interrupt, it sends a message: My voice matters more than yours. Holding back creates space for true understanding. Try waiting until they finish, then take a breath before responding.

- **Avoiding Personal Attacks:** There's a big difference between saying "I feel neglected" and "You don't care about me." One opens a door; the other slams it. When you go after your partner's character, the conversation stops being about the issue and starts being about defending self-worth.

- **Using "I" Statements:** This old communication tip still holds up. "I feel…" focuses on your emotional experience. It's vulnerable. It takes ownership. It invites connection. Compare "You never think about me" with "I feel forgotten when plans are made without me."

- **Taking Responsibility:** Admitting your part in the conflict doesn't mean taking all the blame. It just means being honest. "I could've brought this up earlier" or "I know I was distant too" helps shift the tone from confrontation to collaboration.

Why Respect Matters:

- **It Builds Trust:** Respect creates safety. And emotional safety is the soil where trust grows. When someone knows you'll treat them with dignity even when you're hurt or angry, they're more likely to stay open and engaged.

- **It Encourages Vulnerability**: People shut down when they feel judged. They open up when they feel accepted. Respect says, You're safe here, even when we disagree.

- **It Reduces Defensiveness:** Most of us aren't wired to respond calmly to criticism, even well-meaning feedback. But if the conversation is rooted in mutual respect, the tension drops, and genuine dialogue becomes possible.

Active Listening: The Art of Truly Hearing Your Partner

Listening isn't passive. It's not just sitting silently while the other person speaks. Real listening, active listening, requires energy, presence, and humility.

Think about the last time you felt truly heard. What made that moment stick? Chances are, it wasn't just that someone listened. It's that they got it. They didn't try to fix you. They didn't dismiss your feelings. They sat with you in the mess and said, "I hear you."

How to Practice Active Listening:

- **Give Your Full Attention:** That means no scrolling, no glancing at the clock, no distracted nods. Make eye contact. Let your body language signal, I'm here, I'm with you.

- **Show You're Listening:** You don't have to stay silent. A well-timed "Mm-hmm," or "That makes sense," goes a long way. It tells your partner they aren't speaking into a void.

- **Reflect and Paraphrase:** When you say, "So what I'm hearing is...," you're not being robotic, you're checking for clarity and showing you care. Even if you didn't get it quite right, your partner will likely clarify, which deepens the dialogue.

- **Ask Clarifying Questions:** If something's unclear or emotionally loaded, gently ask for more. "When you say you feel distant, do you mean emotionally or physically?" Or, "What part of that interaction felt most painful to you?"

- **Avoid Planning Your Response:** This one's hard. When you're upset or defensive, your brain starts writing your comeback before your partner even finishes. But try to pause. Just absorb their words. You'll be surprised how often your planned response changes once you truly understand what's being said.

The Power of Reflective Listening:

Let's look at a quick example:

- Partner: "Lately I feel like I'm carrying everything at home, and it's exhausting."
- You: "So you're feeling overwhelmed and maybe a bit alone in managing things?"

This simple reflection says, I see you. I'm trying to get it right. That, in itself, can be healing, even before a solution is found.

Dealing with Strong Emotions During Difficult Conversations

No matter how skilled or kind you are, emotions will rise. That's not a failure, it's a sign that something matters.

The key isn't to eliminate emotion, but to stay present with it without letting it take over. To learn the difference between feeling your feelings and acting them out.

1. **Take a Pause:**

    Sometimes things heat up faster than we can manage. And sometimes, stepping away for a moment is the most respectful thing you can do.

Say something like: "I'm feeling really overwhelmed right now. I want to keep talking, but I need a short break to calm down."

This isn't avoidance, it's stewardship of the conversation. Just make sure to circle back when you're both more grounded.

2. **Breathe and Centre Yourself:**

It might sound simple, but intentional breathing changes everything. When your chest tightens and your throat constricts, taking three slow breaths tells your body, You're safe. It quiets your nervous system and helps you respond with wisdom instead of reactivity.

3. **Acknowledge the Emotions:**

Ignoring feelings doesn't make them go away. In fact, they usually get louder. Instead, try naming what's happening inside you:

- "I'm feeling angry, but I'm trying to stay open."
- "These hurts more than I expected, and I want to stay with you through it."

When you name an emotion, it stops controlling you. It becomes something you're experiencing, not something you are.

There's a moment in nearly every difficult conversation where you get to decide: will I Armor up and protect myself, or will I soften and lean in? That moment is the turning point.

Healthy relationships aren't built on always agreeing or avoiding conflict. They're built on the how, how we speak when we're hurting, how we listen when we're tired, how we show up when things feel messy and unsure.

So, the next time a hard conversation comes up, don't panic. Take a breath. Remember that connection isn't lost in conflict, it's deepened through it, if you stay present, respectful, and open-hearted.

Because underneath the tension is usually a question waiting to be answered: Do you still see me? Do you still care?

And every "I'm listening" is a quiet yes.

The Role of Constructive Feedback in Conflict Resolution

Conflict in relationships isn't a sign of failure, it's a sign that you're two different people trying to walk through life together. That's not easy. When emotions get tangled and things feel tense, it's tempting to retreat into silence or, on the other end of the spectrum, say things you don't mean just to make your point land harder. But there's a quieter power in approaching these moments with intention, through something many of us weren't really taught how to do well: giving and receiving constructive feedback.

Constructive feedback isn't about correcting someone or pointing out all the ways they've let you down. It's about showing up to the conversation with hope, that things can be better, that you're willing to grow together, and that you're choosing the relationship, not just the win. It asks us to speak in a way that doesn't tear down but builds something stronger in its place.

Picture this: You've been waiting for your partner to come home all evening. Dinner's gone cold, you're feeling overlooked, and all the disappointment starts to boil up. They finally walk through the door, apologetic but tired. You could lash out, "You always do this. You never think about how your actions affect me." And maybe that would feel justified in the moment. But would it create the kind of change you actually want?

What if, instead, you said something like, "When you don't let me know you'll be late, I feel dismissed, like my time doesn't matter." It's a subtle shift, but a powerful one. You're not attacking them, you're inviting them into your emotional world. You're showing vulnerability instead of building a wall. That's the kind of feedback that makes someone want to respond with care rather than defensiveness.

There's also something deeply human about pairing honesty with a path forward. If you're going to bring up a problem, don't stop there, light the way to a better version of the situation. You might say, "It would mean a lot to me if, next time, you could just send a quick text when your plans change. That way I can adjust, and I won't spend the whole evening wondering." See how that opens the door? You're not just expressing frustration, you're showing them how to love you better.

But offering feedback doesn't always mean being soft. It means being intentional. You can be firm without being harsh, and you can still hold someone accountable while speaking with kindness. One of the most effective ways to do this is by acknowledging what's going right. "I know you're under a lot of pressure at work, and I see how hard you're trying. I just miss you. I want to make sure we're still making space for each other."

These kinds of conversations don't just help solve individual issues, they shift the tone of the whole relationship. They create a culture of mutual respect and growth, where both people feel safe enough to speak up and humble enough to listen.

And that brings us to the other side of the coin: receiving feedback.

This is where things often get tricky. Most of us have an inner reflex that kicks in the moment we feel criticized. We interrupt, get defensive, or try to explain why they're wrong. But the truth is, when someone we care about is brave enough to tell us how our behaviour has affected them, the most powerful response we can offer is openness.

That might look like taking a breath and just listening. Not planning your comeback. Not mentally constructing your defence. Just staying present and trying to hear the heart behind their words.

Let's say your partner says, "I felt hurt when you didn't include me in that decision." Even if your intentions were good, even if you think they're overreacting, it's not about who's right. It's about whether you're willing to understand how your actions landed on the other side.

You could say, "I didn't realize that made you feel left out. I'm really sorry. That wasn't my intention, but I hear you, and I want to do better." That kind of acknowledgment creates a bridge. It reassures your partner that their feelings matter, even if you don't fully agree with their interpretation. It shows humility, and humility is magnetic in conflict.

Sometimes, feedback won't be as clear as you'd like. That's okay. Instead of guessing or reacting, you can gently ask for more clarity. "Can you help me understand what you needed in that moment?" or "What would have made you feel more supported?"

These kinds of questions don't just defuse tension, they deepen intimacy. They show that you're not just trying to move past the problem quickly but that you're genuinely invested in understanding your partner's experience.

Still, even with all the tools in the world, some conversations can take a turn. Maybe emotions run high, voices get louder, and suddenly, you're both fighting to be heard instead of trying to hear each other. This is when emotional self-regulation becomes not just helpful but essential.

In these moments, the bravest thing you can do might be to pause. Take a breath. Remind yourself that this isn't about winning, it's about reconnecting. It's about protecting the relationship, even if you disagree.

Speaking calmly doesn't mean suppressing your feelings. It means choosing how you express them. Slowing down your speech, grounding your thoughts before responding, these are small acts that have big impact. They prevent you from saying things you can't take back.

And when the urge to blame bubbles up, try to pivot toward curiosity. Instead of, "You never listen to me," try, "I'm struggling to feel heard right now. Can we slow down and try again?" That shift in language moves the focus from attack to resolution.

There will be times, too, when you just don't see eye to eye. And that's okay. Not every disagreement needs to be resolved in perfect alignment. Sometimes, agreeing to disagree can be the healthiest choice. It's not about giving up, it's about honouring each other's differences without turning them into battlegrounds.

The real magic happens not in avoiding conflict, but in how we move through it. When both partners commit to staying open, kind, and solution-oriented, even when it's uncomfortable, that's where trust grows. That's where love deepens.

At the end of the day, constructive feedback isn't just a communication tool. It's an expression of love. It says, "I care enough about this relationship to name what's hard, and I trust you enough to believe we can grow through it." It's not always easy. But the relationships that thrive are the ones where both people are willing to be honest, humble, and human.

So the next time you're navigating a tough conversation, remember: it's not about having the perfect words. It's about bringing your whole self to the moment, messy emotions, imperfect phrasing, and all, with a willingness to listen and a desire to understand. That's where real connection lives.

In the next chapter, we'll take this further by exploring how to build communication habits that support your relationship every day, not just during moments of tension. Because healthy relationships aren't built in crises; they're built in the ordinary, in the quiet moments where understanding becomes the default and not the exception.

CHAPTER SIX

BUILDING HEALTHY COMMUNICATION HABITS FOR LONG-TERM SUCCESS

I n long-term relationships, it's easy to think that the big conversations, those tearful confessions, passionate debates, or milestone-defining talks, are the ones that shape your connection. And while those moments certainly matter, what often gets overlooked is the quiet, everyday rhythm of how we talk to each other. The way we check in over dinner, the patience we offer in disagreement, the way we listen when we're tired or distracted, all of these small habits slowly build the emotional climate of a relationship.

Think of communication like the heartbeat of your relationship. You don't always notice it, but it keeps everything alive. And when it's off, when conversations are strained, or silence lingers a little too long, you can feel the tension, even if nothing dramatic has happened. That's why building healthy communication habits isn't just about solving problems. It's about creating an environment where both partners feel safe, seen, and supported, every day, not just during crisis.

Let's explore two foundational habits that help cultivate this kind of relationship: regular emotional check-ins and a ritual for resolving conflict with grace.

The Power of Regular Check-Ins

Let's start with something deceptively simple: the check-in.

It's easy to underestimate this habit. After all, how much can a ten-minute conversation really do? But here's the thing, relationships don't unravel in one big fight. They unravel quietly, in the spaces where resentment goes unspoken, where loneliness hides under daily routine, and where love gets buried under logistics.

Why Regular Check-Ins Matter

- **Prevent Small Issues from Escalating**

  Imagine you keep stubbing your toe on the same corner of the couch. You don't say anything at first, maybe it's not a big deal. But over time, it starts to hurt. The bruises build up. By the tenth time, you're furious... not just at the couch, but at yourself for not moving it. That's how small relational issues work too. Left unspoken, they quietly bruise our connection. Regular check-ins are like moving the couch before you hurt yourself again.

- **Foster Emotional Intimacy**

  It's easy to talk about what's for dinner or who's picking up the kids. It's harder to say, "I've been feeling off lately and I don't really know why." But these are the conversations where intimacy lives, not in solving everything, but in being willing to show up honestly. When both people feel like they have a safe space to share their inner world, connection deepens.

- **Maintain Connection Through Life's Busyness**

  Life doesn't slow down for relationships. But a weekly check-in can be a small act of rebellion against the chaos, a way of saying, "You still matter, even in the middle of all this." It doesn't have to be a heavy or serious time; sometimes, just asking, "How's your heart this week?" can open the door to meaningful connection.

How to Conduct Effective Check-Ins

- **Choose a Consistent Time**

  Consistency is key. Maybe it's Sunday evenings after dinner, or Friday mornings before the world wakes up. What matters is that you both know this is your time. Treat it like an appointment you don't cancel, because the health of your relationship deserves that kind of priority.

- **Use Open-Ended Questions**

  Avoid yes/no questions like "Are you okay?" Instead, try:
    - "What's been on your mind lately?"
    - "Is there anything I've done this week that you appreciated, or that bothered you?"
    - "How can I support you better right now?"

  These kinds of questions invite reflection and give your partner space to share what they might not otherwise say.

- **Express Appreciation**

  Don't just talk about what needs fixing. Celebrate what's going well. Tell your partner something they did that made you feel loved or seen. Gratitude shifts the tone of the conversation and reinforces your emotional bond.

- **Be Honest and Vulnerable**

  A check-in isn't about pretending everything's fine. It's okay to say, "I've been feeling distant," or "I've been carrying some stress and I think it's showing up in how I talk to you." Vulnerability doesn't always come easily, but it builds trust in a way that surface-level conversation can't.

Creating a Communication Ritual for Conflict Resolution

Of course, not every conversation is warm and fuzzy. Conflict is inevitable in any relationship. But it's not the presence of conflict that determines a couple's strength, it's how they handle it. And often, the difference between constructive and destructive conflict comes down to habits.

When you have a shared ritual for working through disagreements, you give your relationship something incredibly valuable: structure in the chaos. A kind of emotional compass that says, "Even when we're upset, we know how to find our way back to each other."

Why a Conflict Resolution Ritual Is Important

- **Reduces Reactivity**

  We all have our triggers, words that hit a nerve, tones that make us shut down, or situations that bring up old wounds. A ritual helps create space between the trigger and the reaction. It's like installing a pause button where you'd normally lash out or withdraw.

- **Promotes Fairness**

  In heated moments, one person can easily dominate the conversation, talking louder, interrupting, or dismissing.

But when you agree ahead of time on a process, both people are more likely to feel heard and valued.

- **Strengthens Trust**

  When your partner knows that even in conflict, you won't abandon or belittle them, that you'll stay at the table, emotionally and literally, it builds deep trust. You become each other's safe place, even when things are hard.

Steps for a Healthy Conflict Resolution Ritual

- **Pause Before Reacting**

  When emotions flare, it's okay to take a moment. Say something like, "I want to talk about this, but I need five minutes to collect my thoughts." Use the time to breathe, go for a walk, or just cool down. It's not about avoiding the issue, it's about making space for your best self to show up.

- **Use "I" Statements**

  Blame puts people on the defensive. But owning your feelings with "I" statements invites empathy.

    o Instead of: "You never listen to me."

    o Try: "I feel overlooked when I don't feel heard."

  This small shift can lower defensiveness and open the door to real understanding.

- **Take Turns Speaking**
- Try using a "talking object" to designate who has the floor— yes, it might feel silly at first, but it works. When one person

speaks, the other listens without interrupting. Then switch. This structure slows down the conversation and ensures both voices are truly heard.

- **Offer Solutions, Not Just Complaints**
Complaining without proposing change can make your partner feel powerless. After both of you share how you feel, ask: "What can we do differently next time?" or "How could we both feel more supported in this area?" Focusing on solutions turns conflict into collaboration.

- **End on a Positive Note**
Conflict isn't just about fixing problems, it's an opportunity to grow closer. Once the air is cleared, take a moment to reconnect. A hug, a shared laugh, or a simple, "I appreciate that we can talk about hard things," can go a long way in restoring your emotional bond.

Communication as a Daily Act of Love

In the end, building healthy communication habits isn't about becoming perfect communicators. It's about committing to stay present, to keep showing up, and to value your connection enough to tend to it, on ordinary days, during hard conversations, and in all the in-between moments.

Communication isn't just about words. It's about tone, timing, and the intention behind what we say. It's about listening with curiosity instead of preparing your next point. It's about knowing that when your partner speaks, they're not just reporting facts, they're offering a glimpse into their inner world. And when you respond with care, you become someone they can trust with that world.

That's the kind of intimacy that doesn't fade with time. It deepens. It steadies you through storms. It reminds you, again and again, that you are not alone in this life.

So, whether you're beginning a relationship or rebuilding one, start here, with regular check-ins, honest conflict rituals, and a willingness to speak and listen with your whole heart. These habits may be simple, but over time, they become sacred. And in the quiet, steady practice of healthy communication, love finds its deepest roots.

The Role of Non-Verbal Communication in Building Connection

It's funny how we can say so much without saying anything at all.

You've probably felt it before, that moment when someone says "I'm fine," but their crossed arms and distant stare tell you everything you need to know. Or when a loved one doesn't say a word but reaches over to squeeze your hand at just the right moment. That one gesture can say more than a hundred comforting sentences.

That's the heart of non-verbal communication. It's not just the background noise of our conversations, it is the conversation, at least part of it. In fact, research often suggests that a huge portion of what we communicate happens non-verbally. That means how we say something, the tilt of our head, the softness of our tone, or the way we lean in to listen, can completely reshape the meaning of our words.

In relationships, this becomes even more important. Whether we're aware of it or not, we're always tuning in to each other's cues. And if we want to truly connect, not just co-exist or get through the day, we have to learn how to be fluent in this silent language.

How Non-Verbal Cues Impact Communication

- **Tone of Voice:**
  Have you ever said something completely neutral like, "What are you doing?" and had it received either playfully, angrily, or suspiciously, depending on the tone? That's the power of inflection. A loving tone, even in disagreement, can

change the temperature of a whole conversation. It signals, "I'm here with you, not against you." On the other hand, when our tone becomes sharp or distant, it can feel like a wall is going up, even when we don't mean for it to.

Tone is often where we reveal what we're really feeling before we've figured it out ourselves. That's why it's worth paying attention to. If your tone suddenly shifts, it's not about performing the "right" version of yourself, it's about noticing what's going on inside. Am I speaking from love? Or am I letting frustration speak for me?

- **Body Language:**

Sometimes we listen with our whole bodies. Leaning in, nodding, relaxing our shoulders, all these subtle shifts say, I'm present. I'm listening. I care. Think about the difference between having a conversation with someone who's scrolling through their phone versus someone who's turned toward you, making gentle eye contact, nodding slowly as you speak. You feel the difference in your body.

Closed-off body language, even when unintentional, can send a message of disinterest or defence. Crossed arms, avoiding eye contact, turning away, these may just be signs of stress or distraction, but to a partner, they can feel like rejection. That's not to say we should perform openness all the time, but it helps to be aware. Especially in hard conversations, softening your posture or simply facing your partner can make it easier for both of you to stay grounded.

- **Physical Touch:**

  Touch might be the most primal form of communication we have. A hug when words fail. A hand on the back during a hard moment. Even the gentle brush of a thumb while holding hands. These gestures often say what words cannot: I see you. I'm with you. You're not alone.

  In times of stress, touch can be a bridge back to safety. In moments of celebration, it can magnify joy. Of course, not everyone has the same comfort level with physical affection, and that's okay. What matters is finding the kind of touch that feels connecting for both of you. Sometimes it's not grand gestures, it's the small, everyday touches that create a rhythm of love.

How to Improve Your Non-Verbal Communication

- **Be Aware of Your Tone:**

  Tone awareness isn't about being overly cautious or fake. It's more like emotional mindfulness. When you notice your voice getting louder, sharper, or colder, it might be your inner self asking for attention. Take a breath. Ground yourself. Is this tone helping the conversation, or building a wall?

A calm, gentle tone can act like a balm, even when discussing tough topics. It doesn't mean you can't be firm or express hurt. It just means you're choosing to speak in a way that invites connection instead of defensiveness.

- **Practice Open Body Language:**

  This doesn't require a mirror or a checklist. It's more about being present. Are you facing your partner? Are your hands relaxed? Are your eyes meeting theirs, or are you somewhere else entirely, lost in thought or on your phone?

  Small shifts in body language can do a lot to build trust. Sitting beside someone instead of across from them during a tough talk. Uncrossing your arms. Making room for them, literally and emotionally. These gestures tell your partner: You're safe with me. I want to hear you.

- **Use Touch to Reassure:**

  Sometimes in the middle of an argument, the kindest thing you can do is reach out. Not with solutions. Not with words. Just with presence. A hand on the knee. A shoulder leaned against theirs. If it's welcome and safe, this kind of non-verbal gesture can shift the whole emotional tone.

It's not about fixing anything. It's about anchoring back to love.

The Importance of Mutual Support and Encouragement

There's something deeply healing about being seen, and still loved.

In a thriving relationship, love doesn't just look like affection or compatibility. It looks like support. Like having someone in your corner when you're afraid. Like being cheered on when you try something new, and comforted when things fall apart. When encouragement becomes a habit, it builds something unshakable between you: resilience.

Why Support is Crucial

- **Boosts Confidence:**
  When your partner believes in you, it does something to your insides. You start to see yourself through their eyes. That encouragement, even when quiet or subtle, helps you take leaps you might not otherwise risk. It tells you, You're not doing this alone. And that can be the difference between giving up and trying again.

- **Fosters Teamwork:**

At its best, a relationship isn't a competition—it's a collaboration. When both partners are encouraging each other, it stops being about who's doing more or less and starts becoming a dance. You look out for each other. You fill in the gaps when the other is tired. You show up.

Support doesn't always mean fixing things, it often means simply being a steady presence. A witness. A teammate.

- **Strengthens Emotional Resilience:**
Life gets hard sometimes. Illness, job loss, family stress, internal battles, none of us are immune. But what softens the blows is knowing someone's in it with you. When your partner wraps you in words of comfort or quietly holds space for your pain, it plants seeds of resilience.

You both start to believe: We can get through this. Together.

How to Provide Support in Communication

- **Celebrate Successes:**
Don't underestimate the power of pausing to say, "I'm proud of you." Whether your partner nailed a big presentation or just made it through a rough day, acknowledgment is oxygen. It keeps dreams alive.

Support means celebrating the little wins, not just the grand ones. A kind word. A smile. A hug after a long day. These small rituals of encouragement can become the glue that holds you together.

- **Offer Encouragement in Difficult Times:**

When your partner is struggling, don't rush to solve it. Just be there. Remind them of their strength. Tell them you believe in them, not in a performative way, but in the way you lean in when they need you most.

Even saying, "This is hard, and I'm right here with you," can be enough. Often, people don't need answers, they need assurance.

- **Create a Safe Space for Vulnerability:**

Real support means welcoming your partner's whole self, not just the polished version. When you create space for your partner to be fully themselves, to cry, to admit fears, to dream out loud, it deepens your connection.

This kind of safety takes time, but it's built through everyday choices. Not laughing at their dreams. Not minimizing their emotions. Listening with your heart, not just your ears. Being someone they can come home to emotionally, not just physically.

Love is not just built in the grand, sweeping moments. It's woven together through the subtle, silent, and steady choices we make, especially in how we communicate.

When we pay attention to our non-verbal cues, we become more attuned to what our partner really needs, not just what they say they need. And when we offer consistent support and encouragement, we build a relationship that doesn't just survive life's ups and downs, it grows stronger because of them.

So the next time you're sitting beside your partner in silence, remember: even that silence is saying something. Let it say I'm here. I see you. I care.

As we continue forward, we'll explore how to not only stay connected but to grow together, to nurture a relationship that deepens with time, rich with the kind of love that endures through every season of life.

CONCLUSION

S
o here we are, at the end, but also at the beginning. That's the thing about love. Just when you think you've figured it out, it stretches. Deepens. Invites you into new territory. And that's part of the beauty, isn't it? Love isn't a final destination. It's a living, breathing relationship that asks you to show up, again and again, with intention and humility.

Throughout this book, we've explored many parts of that journey. We've looked at the way our words can either build bridges or walls. We've seen how silence, when misused, can create distance, and how listening, when done with care, can dissolve it. At the heart of it all is something deceptively simple: communication. But not just any kind. It's the kind that requires us to be both brave and gentle. To speak honestly, and to receive honesty without defence. To make room for the messiness of real emotions, and to choose connection over control.

That's what lasting love is built on.

You've probably noticed that great communication in relationships isn't about fancy language or perfect timing. It's not about never disagreeing. It's not even about always knowing the right thing to say. It's about a mindset, an orientation toward each other that says, I care enough to stay present. I care enough to try again. I care enough to keep learning how to love you better.

It's a commitment to the long game.

And if you're here, reading this conclusion, chances are, you're someone who wants that kind of love. Maybe you've already begun cultivating it. Or maybe you've just realized how important it is. Either way, it's worth pausing here to acknowledge how powerful that intention is. It takes courage to look inward. It takes humility to admit you don't have all the answers. It takes maturity to keep showing up, not with a checklist, but with a heart that's open and willing.

Because love, as we've seen, is not static. It grows or it fades. And communication is the sunlight and water it needs to keep growing.

Let's go back for a moment to something subtle but crucial: understanding your communication style, and your partner's. That alone can transform how you relate. When you begin to notice your patterns, how you react when you feel unheard, how your partner tends to express stress, how both of you seek comfort, you start to develop empathy. And empathy, more than any clever technique, is what makes communication meaningful.

It's what softens defensiveness and invites tenderness. It's what turns an argument into a chance to reconnect. When you begin to listen not just for content, but for what's underneath, the fear, the longing, the need for reassurance, everything changes.

We often think of communication as what we say, but more often than not, it's how we show up. Are we interrupting, or leaning in? Are we formulating our reply, or absorbing what's being shared? Are we looking to win the conversation, or understand each other more deeply?

It's a quiet kind of skill, this form of presence. But it's a powerful one. And it builds trust in ways words alone can't.

Think about the moments in your relationship when you've felt most safe. Most seen. Most deeply loved. It probably wasn't because someone had the perfect sentence prepared. It was likely because they stayed with you, in your emotion, your uncertainty, your joy, your pain, and didn't try to fix or change you. That is the heart of real communication. That is what intimacy sounds like.

And let's not forget, too, that this isn't about becoming some flawless version of yourself. Growth doesn't happen in a straight line. Some days you'll be calm and patient. Other days, you'll snap, retreat, or get it completely wrong. That's okay. Because love doesn't ask for perfection. It asks for participation. For effort. For the willingness to come back and try again.

There's something very grounding in that. To know that even when things feel off, or uncertain, or overwhelming, you have tools now. You have awareness. You have language. You have the ability to slow down, to turn toward each other, and to rebuild connection, again and again.

Over time, these choices become a rhythm. A way of life. And that's where the real transformation happens. Because relationships aren't changed by big, dramatic gestures nearly as much as they are shaped by the tiny, consistent ones. The goodnight kisses. The "how was your day?" texts. The shared jokes. The willingness to say, "I hear you, and I care."

It's not about fixing each other. It's about witnessing each other. Growing beside each other. Laughing, stumbling, and returning to love, again and again.

That's what makes a relationship feel safe. That's what creates space for vulnerability. That's what lets love become not just something you feel, but something you do.

And here's something else: the journey of growing as individuals within a relationship is just as important. When you support each other's dreams, when you cheer each other on, when you make space for evolving identities, you're not just maintaining a connection; you're deepening it.

The dance between personal growth and partnership isn't always graceful. Sometimes it looks like tension. Sometimes it means re-learning how to relate. But when you choose to grow together, even your differences can become sources of richness, not resentment.

And don't underestimate the role of joy. The silliness. The inside jokes. The way you look at each other across a crowded room and burst out laughing because of a shared memory. Those light hearted moments are not trivial, they are lifelines. They keep you connected when life gets heavy. They remind you that, even in the hard times, your love still has room for levity.

That's the beauty of lasting love: it holds everything. The depth and the delight. The challenges and the celebrations. The quiet mornings and the tearful nights. And through it all, communication is the thread that ties you together.

Now, as you continue building this love story, whether you're newly together, decades in, or somewhere in between, carry this truth with you: your relationship is worth the effort. It's worth the conversations that stretch you. The apologies that humble you. The new ways of listening that might feel awkward at first but eventually become second nature.

This isn't about having a perfect relationship. It's about having a real one. One where both of you feel seen, heard, and cherished.

One where challenges don't mean the end, but a new beginning. One where growth is shared, love is chosen daily, and communication is a sacred practice, not just a skill.

So, if you're feeling hopeful, good. If you're feeling overwhelmed, that's okay too. What matters most is your willingness to show up. To choose each other. To stay curious. To keep learning.

There will be seasons when the love feels effortless, and seasons when it requires intention. That's normal. That's human. The key is not to panic in the hard seasons, but to remember what brought you here in the first place. To return to your values. To return to each other.

And when in doubt, let kindness be the language you speak. Let grace be the tone you use. Let love, not ego, have the final word.

Thank you for allowing this guide to walk with you. Whether you've read every chapter or skimmed only a few, I hope something in these pages reminded you of your own power to create connection. To love well. To listen fully. To build something beautiful that lasts.

You deserve a relationship that feels like home. One where you can be your whole self and be loved for it. One where growth isn't a threat, but a shared adventure. One where communication isn't a struggle, but a lifeline. One where both of you feel like you belong.

The road ahead will have its bumps. But you now know how to navigate it, with empathy, with courage, and with heart. You have the tools. You have the insight. And you have the love.

So, take that next step, together.

The process will work if you do the process.

Here's to lasting love. And to you, because you're worth it.

www.ingramcontent.com/pod-product-compliance
Lightning Source LLC
Chambersburg PA
CBHW060031050426
42448CB00012B/2951